# 28 WAYS TO SERIOUSLY SAVE MONEY

By Kevin Robins

*How to seriously
save money; written
with the best
intentions.*

*Dedicated to Miss
Robins.*

# FOREWORD

In this book I want to share my ideas and theories which have helped me, and I hope will help you in order to seriously save you money.

It will involve a combination of being sensible with everyday purchases, taking some risks, but at the right time.

It could show you where potentially cutting some corners and saving money on the necessities in life which we all cannot avoid, but can all save a bit of money on.

My advice and tips will hopefully help you open your eyes to the possibility of being more financially astute.

This will also guide you towards making the right decisions and explore the prospect of actually saving some money for that metaphorical 'rainy day'.

I will explain in some detail about loans, credit cards, insurances and finances in general. As well as tips on trying to make small changes to your lifestyle which can affect your cash flow such as smoking and drinking.

I will teach you the following; don't be beaten by the system, Don't take the first price that you're given and don't impulse buy!

I want to try to help you change the way in which you think about money, its uses and importance in our everyday lives, and the way in which we use it.

If possible, I want to be able to help you save towards putting a deposit down for a house, car or even just accumulate life savings which will undoubtedly help you later on in life. It is of paramount importance to preserve a minimum amount of savings, which can contribute towards sustaining a future for you and your family

## 1. <u>CUT UP CREDIT CARDS</u>

Credit cards are the ultimate cardinal sin. If you are in the process of trying to get together money so you can save a deposit for a mortgage, you will need to get your credit card, clear the balance and cut it up as soon as you possibly can.

It has been a growing trend in recent times, and especially in the economic climate of the recent past to own a credit card, to make high value purchases and then worry about it later.

There is one important rule that you must always remember when it comes to credit cards and borrowing; If you cannot afford it, you cannot buy it.

An element of discipline must come into the equation. You must also be prepared to put in a lot of hard work and make big sacrifices, as saving money vigorously can be a long and hard road, but as long as you have your goal in mind, you will get there.

If you are already in a position where you have a bad existing credit rating, are already in debt and attempting to pay of what you owe, then you just need to get back to basics.

The best way to get out of credit card debt is to firstly; draw up a personal budget for yourself and allocate as much free money after all allowable expenses as possible. Then secondly, gradually pay off as much off the credit card balance as possible.

It does all sound so simple when its put down in words and its very difficult to not make it sound so patronising, but it really is that simple. It will involve a lot of hard work and dedication, but that's all we need in life to succeed and get what we want. So lets go and get it.

## 2. <u>NO LOANS</u>

A loan is basically a financial institution i.e a bank or building society lending a consumer a fixed amount of money, having an agreement in place to pay the money back over a certain amount of time, with the addition of interest charged for the privilege.

So this is much the same principle as credit cards, meaning that they are an unnecessary burden hanging over your head and something that needs to be brought under control sooner rather than later.

People often just see the figure that they want to borrow, and not the total sum payable at the end of the term. The interest rate on any loan is ludicrous and all banks, loan companies and even worse loan sharks, will feed on the fact that people need the money, and need it now.

Believe it or not, many people actually believe that with credit cards and loans, you don't actually need to pay the money back, which is obviously quite ridiculous. The best thing is to just avoid them as much as possible.

Patience it was once said is a virtue, and its something that needs to be put into practice with finances. Loans will lead you down a long slippery slope into bankruptcy if you are not careful. So buyer beware!

## 3. **NO MOBILE PHONES ON CONTRACTS**

Mobile phone contracts are another con, sugar coated to be made to look like that they are a good deal.

Mobile phone companies are very good at the small print advertising technique. Just because you don't see that small print straight away, it doesn't mean that it's not there!

The average monthly phone contract price is £40. Some newer models are even reaching the bad side of £60, with the pull to the customer being a brand new gadget as a gift for taking out the contract in the first place.

The new generation of smartphones has revolutionised the way in which we use technology now on a daily basis. They are incredible machines capable of doing anything you want them to. But having said this, they are a luxury item.

Luxury items are not necessities, nor are they financially viable when attempting to save money and tighten up the proverbial belts.

Do yourself a favour, and buy a cheap pay as you go phone for less than £30 and keep it for as long as you can. In terms of saving money and drawing up a monthly budget, that average of £40-£60 that you are paying every month on a mobile phone is an astonishing saving which can go towards something far more useful.

Try to think about the bigger picture and in the longer term, look to saving towards that deposit for a house, an investment for life.

## 4. <u>NO CARS ON FINANCE DEALS</u>

A car is something that most people need to be able to get on in every day life. Whether it be the daily commute to work, or picking your kids up from school.

But it's something that can be done on a budget, as with anything else in life. Let's face it, £400 per month for a BMW X5 to sit on the drive every day, only to be used twice for the school rounds each day isn't logical.

If you're going to buy a car make sure that first and foremost that it's safe, reliable and economical. The manufacturer of the car is not as important as most people think, buying a car is completely down to the luck of the draw.

Wherever possible, buy a car by cheque so that it is always a traceable source of funds, for that added piece of mind just incase you encounter any problems with the dealer or private owner.

You must try to avoid buying the big brands as with any consumer product, cars are no different. A cars value will depreciate from the moment you drive it away that first time.

So in order to make the purchase as much of an investment as possible, look towards the Japanese market, they are well made machines, reliable and usually reasonably priced for parts with good sell-on values.

With the ever rising cost of fuel, it is definitely worth buying a diesel car as opposed to petrol. It may be more expensive per litre to buy, Think economical, think practical.

## 5.  SAVE YOUR PENNIES IN A JAR

Out of your monthly cash allowance, don't just disregard the loose change and old shrapnel that weighs down your pockets everyday. If you obtain any coins below a 20p, keep them to one side and put them in a savings jar.

By trying to do this religiously soon adds up and by the end of the month you could find yourself £10 richer, doesn't always seem like a lot at the time but its £120 a year.

Most high street banks will now actually offer a free coin payment service. Whereby you can get together all of your coins and pay them directly into your bank account without being charged commission as is usually the case with machines such as Coin star.

This is such a good way of recycling money, not letting any of it go to waste. You have to remember that it's all money, no matter in what form, whether it be in notes or coins

## 6. DON'T MOVE HOME, IMPROVE YOUR HOME

When you calculate the cost of moving home with all solicitors and estate agent fees considered, if your budget is small then it's worth thinking about the possibility of extending instead. If it's viable, it is definitely worth looking into building a conservatory or extension on your existing property.

Take some time and keep the figure in mind that you're willing or able to spend.

Have a look online and you'll be able to find various companies that work on a supply and fit or supply only basis. Buying online this way you can  save a substantial sum of money.

Make sure you use a registered company with all of the proper credentials required, for piece of mind it is worth a phone call to the regulatory bodies to confirm if these companies are honest members.

If you decide to build an extension of some sort on your property, whether it be a standard domestic extension, conservatory, roof conversion or single dwelling enhancement, make sure you do your homework when looking into who is going to do the work for you.

Search online for a builders credibility and keep it local, there are several websites out there with trusted traders and feedback from previously satisfied clients, which will help you make ane educated decision.

Get in touch with at least two or three local and recommended builders in your area, and ask them around for a free no obligation quotation to carry out the appropriate works.

One of the first rules is to never take the first price that you are given, you will be able to save yourself a lot more money by comparing all of the quotes that you get, knowing full well that you don't have to worry about compromising on the quality of the work, as all of the traders you have considered are fully vetted and recommended by your previously visited websites.

If you cannot afford to pay all of the legal fees, then improving and extending your home for the near future is the way forward.

You will have the potential to add an extra 5%-10% value onto your property, to help you for when you are in a better position financially to move and earn more money on the property in the process.

## 7. QUIT SMOKING

We all understand that smoking is an addiction, and that nicotine like any other drug needs to be taken to feed it, but it is not a good habit for all of the obvious reasons such as the cost implications as well as your health.

As with any other addiction, it costs a lot of money. The cost of cigarettes and tobacco is constantly on the rise, and as we are gradually coming out of the smoking culture as a nation the appeal is no longer there to do it.

The public perception has greatly changed since half a century ago when smoking was actually promoted and glorified.

When you actually sit down and look at figures, it is really quite scary how much smoking as a regular thing actually costs.

An average cost of cigarettes being approximately £4 a pack and this cost as an average will always rise.

A 20-30 a day smoker will get through at least two packets of these daily, equating to over £50 per week, and £200 a month. So with that average cost of £2400 per year, that's when most people really start to take notice.

There is no real advantage to smoking anymore, the fun has been taken out of it for those who claim that they actually enjoy it due to the cost, let alone the health risks for all smokers.

So for that £2400 that you are saving, and the time that you are saving on your life by quitting smoking, it is a sacrifice worth making. Put the money towards a holiday, towards a car or storing it away in savings.

## 8. DRINK LESS ALCOHOL, OR QUIT.

Drinking is another habit that can get out of control in many ways. Some people like to drink after work to unwind, others go for a few drinks on a Friday night after work, and then there are also those that are addicted to it.

Whichever category of drinker that you fall into, and no matter what your alcohol consumption is, it will all cost you money. Alcohol is another expensive consumer product that many people fall into the trap of spending a lot of money on.

With many spirited bottles costing in excess of £20 for the stay at home drinker, and bottles of lager costing in excess of £3 in most bars, it can lead to an expensive night in or out.

As evidence shows with the recent economic downturn, many of the United Kingdoms public houses and drinking clubs have had to close due to lack of custom, with the nation tightening their belts in general, the nightlife culture understandably took a battering.

Britain has gained a reputation in recent years for breeding a generation of alcohol-loving degenerates. It has become very common for a young twenty-something to frequently spend upwards of £50 per night on a social night out on the tiles, and this has been where a lot of people go wrong, and where they find it difficult to keep to some sort of budget.

Try as much as you can to limit your drinking to significant social gatherings or occasions only, as frequent drinkers will often find themselves spending in excess of £200 per month on the alcohol, and when you think about it, any money spent in great quantities on alcohol is a great waste, as you have nothing to show for it, it's consumed as quickly as the money is spent.

## 9. SET A MONTHLY PERSONAL ALLOWANCE.

If you are one of these people that find it hard to keep the cash that's in your pocket because of the temptation to keep spending, then think about giving yourself a personal monthly allowance.

On payday go to the ATM and draw out a minimum sum of money for emergencies that will get you out of trouble at the last minute.

It's advisable to take out between £15-£20 a month and keep it in your wallet. Whatever you do, try not to spend over it! Spend it as you wish, within reason but keep a lid on it as it's so easy for it to get out of control.

Having a level of discipline with money is essential to be able to save it, so by testing yourself on a monthly basis you can see just how far a small amount of money will go because you have put a limit on it, so you will eventually find yourself not buying unnecessary items, as you are fully aware that you are at risk of reaching your allowance sooner than you would like.

But by all means don't spend all of the allowance if you don't need to, keep it to one side and let it roll over to the next month so that you aren't using as much money each month for the allowance.

**10. PUT A STOP TO LUXURY PURCHASES.**

Luxury purchases should remain exactly as they are, a luxury until it is something that you can actually afford. At tough times it is especially difficult to stick to a budget when it seems like you are not getting anywhere.

You feel as though you need to treat yourself, and then before you know it you've already spent savings or a personal allowance on a luxury item or an electronic gadget, which probably won't ever get used.

 Refrain from buying unnecessary kitchen appliances such as coffee and smoothie makers, espresso machines, doughnut makers and suchlike. The electronics industry also makes a killing on Blu-Ray DVD players, 3DTV's and Recorders. These and many more items of the same mould are items that we can all live without while things are a bit tight and you need to count those pennies.

At the end of the day we all need something to look forward to, to aspire to and to save towards. So a luxury purchase is no different. If we bought everything that we ever wanted, then where would our drive be? We need that determination and willing in order to succeed.

## 11. MAKE CHANGES TO THE WEEKLY SHOP.

It is always a good idea to get organised with anything to do with money. The more organised you are, the more money you will save. It's a fact, financial planning is key. Set yourself a budget for weekly shopping, or a monthly one and make sure you do not go over that allowance.

Avoid the brands for certain products, because if you are really honest with yourself you will know that there is no real compromise on the quality. It's important to remember that you don't always get what you pay for. Why pay over the odds for toilet roll and detergents? Why be ripped off for cleaning materials and the weekly essentials just because of a name?

It's time to start thinking logically. Draw up a list of the essential products that you usually buy, and draft in the other items that will last the longest and go the furthest. It will be products for adding to meals and as side dishes, low value but high return if you like.

Buy as many tins and frozen foods as possible, bearing in mind that you want items that will last longer. Refrain from buying too much fresh and refrigerated goods as you will be amazed at how much people throw away at the end of the week, money literally wasted.

Preserve and freeze what you can, and use the leftovers from main meals and put them towards lunches for anyone that goes to work or school etc, don't let anything go to waste.

The last thing to bear in mind is how far you actually have to go to your nearest supermarket. Most people live on average 5-7 miles away from a superstore, so at a minimum based on a weekly shop you will be driving an extra 20 miles per month, and with the ever rising cost of fuel it is worth looking into the cost of online shopping delivery, and seeing what you are better off doing. You could be better off this way as you are potentially saving money and definitely saving time

## 12. REDUCE OR REMOVE TV BOX SUBSCRIPTIONS

This is another scandalous business of high proportion. So many people pay a significant amount of money each month on TV boxes such as Tivo, Sky+ and any other cable subscriptions. Many of these providers asking for in excess of £50 a month to enjoy the additional channels available to them.

With these products you need to sit down and weigh up the options, and look into the cost implications involved when signing up for a new TV package deal. Most of these package subscriptions are not worth the money they are priced at so be very careful when you decide which deal to go for. Ideally you should try to resort to different ways of watching digital channels.

Other options include Freeview, which is obviously a much cheaper and easier option. A plug and play box which you just pay the one off price for the box and away you go. The other alternative is the Freesat box. As long as you have a satellite dish it works just as the same principle as Freeview.

Freesat actually provides you with more channels with more variety. This way you will pay a one off charge for the price of the box and no more. There are no more additional costs, and you will also benefit from a range of features that a Freesat box offers, such as a programme recording facility and a favourites scheduling option.

These are the kinds of cuts that you need to be making from your monthly outgoings that contribute towards your end-game savings plan.

## 13. ALWAYS NEGOTIATE ON HIGH VALUE PURCHASES.

One important thing to remember is that when you are in a position when you need to make a high value purchase i.e Appliances, Cars, Carpets and Furniture, you should never take the first price that you are given.

You need to be able to spend the time and compare prices yourself, go into different stores and negotiate on prices.

Get like-for-like quotations on the same products from all competitors offering the same product. It may take some time, but it will save you money.

Shops will often say that they cannot better the price that is on the shelf and that there is nothing they can offer you to clinch the deal.

This is all untrue, you have to play them at their own game. Take all relevant paperwork with you such as quotes from competitors and play hard ball with them.

No company wants to lose a sale, especially when they have spent a lot of time with you, trying to sell you the product and highlight all of the benefits that the product has to offer.

## 14. CANCEL MAGAZINE SUBSCRIPTIONS

Magazine subscriptions whether they be weekly or monthly are sometimes a cost that people who have them will often completely forget about and not even consider how much they are actually spending on them each period.

You need to establish first and foremost whether having the subscriptions in the first instance is something you can do without or not, and then decide if you are actually happy to pay for it, because if you are not, then it is something you need to put a stop to and begin to make savings.

Quite often there are situations where people are conned into buying a magazine online thinking that they are just buying one issue, not knowing that they have actually entered into a contract and therefore signed up for a continuous subscription which can often fall under their radars, as the amounts are not always great but will obviously add up in costs, so always be very wary of what you are signing yourself up for and check your bank statements regularly.

Most magazines and newspapers are all available online now so there is no need to get yourself tangled in a web full of nasty subscriptions and tie-ins which will eat away at your bank balance each month.

Most subscriptions in general can be very difficult to get out of, and quite often leave the buyer out of pocket. There is normally some kind of small print that tends not to be seen by consumers and this will often state that you will have to submit a request in writing to the magazine itself, and state that you wish to stop your membership and officially give notice of your leaving.

## 15. NO STORE CARDS

Store cards are quite possibly one of the most expensive forms of debt that consumers can fall into. With common interest rates of store cards well over 10%, they are a very difficult payment facility to manage.

Typically the larger department stores will offer incentives and many different types of store cards with added bonuses dependant on the spend of the card, but they are all essentially a gimmick that lands the majority of consumers into debt and seriously affects their credit rating.

One of the serious issues surrounding store cards and the way that they are sold is to do with the sales assistants in the department stores who sell them to you.

Most of these members of staff are not too well informed of all of the dangers involved and what the financial implications may be, as the sales staff may just be on a commission drive to see who can sell the most store cards in a month, for example.

So you must always be aware of anyone who tries to sell you anything that are not educated enough on the product that they are selling you.

Many consumers have found that they struggle to keep up with the payments of store cards and end up consolidating their debts into other so-called manageable loans so that they will find it easier to pay off. However, doing this has proved to have a severely poor effect on their credit rating which in turn hinders their chances of securing a mortgage loan.

## 16. DIESEL CARS

Most people don't like the idea of diesel cars because they think they are too noisy and that the fuel itself is far too expensive when compared to petrol fuels and cars.

But the reality is that you will get a lot more for your money and you will maximise your cars performance.

Diesel cars are will actually run for a lot longer than a petrol car will, and have the capacity to drive for well over 200,000 miles in a lot of cases, if looked after and serviced regularly.

If you are planning to keep your car for a period of several years or so, then getting a diesel car will save you a lot of money overall.

Diesel fuel is marginally more expensive these days, what with the constant rising fuel costs anyway. It's also a fact that the diesel fuel will last at least a third longer than what petrol will.

Tax is generally cheaper on diesel cars with smaller engines as the emissions are a lot fewer also.

## 17. INSULATE YOUR HOME EFFECTIVELY

In the current economic climate it has proved prudent to invest in your existing property.

If you are a homeowner and you try to do what you can to retain the value of your property, look into the possibility of renovating it if possible, which will give you the opportunity to also improve the energy performance of the house overall.

One of the best ways available to you to economically maximise the energy performance of your home is to insulate it wherever possible.

One of the most common ways of insulating a property is to install fibreglass rockwall insulation and pack it into the rafters of your roof, usually from inside the loft. There are various other types of this insulation available, such as foil rolls which can be stapled onto the rafters in a similar manner to the fibreglass insulation.

Another popular way in which you can insulate your home is to bring in specialist insulation companies which are available to provide an insulation pumping service.

These companies can pump the insulation into your cavity walls and other soffit areas around your home. These are an ideal solution to making the most of the energy performance that your home provides.

Ensure that you have adequate draught exclusions around all doorways, especially to your main external doors to the front and back of your property (if applicable).

Make sure you task yourself with other simple little changes that you can make which could have a significant positive impact, such as ensuring all of your internal doors are lined properly, shut whenever possible and that all windows are sealed properly, with no air getting through.

## 18. RECYCLE DVD'S, CD'S FOR CASH

Another one of the most popular ways to raise small amounts of cash is to recycle a lot of your unwanted and unused DVDs, CDs and console games.

If you are looking to raise a bit of extra cash, this is an ideal way of doing it. Especially if you are looking to save for some spending money for a holiday.

Have a look through your collection of DVDs, CDs and games. Sometimes its hard to part with things that you may have had for a long time, but if you know that you will not use them anymore, then you need to make the decision and sell them.

It's a great way of saving money while at the same time you will also be condensing down the rubbish that is in your room and creating some more space for you.

To ensure that you get the best deal possible, have a look around the internet and search for the sites that offer these selling online facilities, and compare the prices that they will offer you.

The process of selling your unwanted items is pretty simple then, all you need to do is pack them all up and get them ready in a box, and usually the website that you use will supply you with a pre-paid envelope or stamp which you put on the box. Take it down to your nearest post office and get a receipt.

You will already have given details as to whether you want to receive a cheque or money by online transfer, so then you just need to wait for the money to come in.

## 19. SELL UNWANTED JEWELLERY

In the past few years the market for unwanted and second hand jewellery has increased rapidly.

There are now many options available to you when dealing with unwanted jewellery in the event that you are strapped for cash and need to earn a quick bit of money. As there are now many outlets to sell through.

One of the main reasons for the high demand in gold and silver is the huge increase in price. Most high street jewellers and second hand merchants will make cash offers, which is based on the consistency, purity and weight of the gold or silver items.

It provides an ideal opportunity to raise some extra capital if required, from items that may not even be used at home.

So always bear in mind that if you have some items of jewellery lying around the house that you know that you have no intention of wearing, get them all together and cash them in.

## 20. BUY YOUR HOME, DON'T RENT

Buying a house is the single biggest purchase and investment that a person can make in their lifetime.

It is a very big commitment and one that shouldn't be taken lightly, but it is something that should be seriously considered.

It has been recently proven that over the course of an average persons lifetime, they will save over £200,000 if they buy a house rather than renting one.

With many people taking the option not to buy, as they think it is too much of a tie in, they are handing over excess amounts of money each year unnecessarily.

The investment element to purchasing a property is a great benefit, as it provides financial security during tough times when people may need to borrow money for instance, they can borrow against some of the equity in their mortgage.

There are several benefits over buying a house rather than renting.

As previously mentioned is the benefit of being able to borrow against the equity, but also the payments are flexible and tailored to you, depending on what mortgage you have.

Whereas, when you are renting a property, the rental cost will always be on the increase in line with inflation, as opposed to mortgage repayments which will gradually decrease throughout its term.

## 21. BULK BUY – WHERE POSSIBLE

This is an ideal opportunity for us as consumers to save good sums of money. The best way that this can be done, and the best explain the type of bulk buying where you can save large sums of money is when you need to buy appliances and furniture.

Along with comparing prices and going from one place to another where you will try to place one place off against the other, the best way to get the best prices from anywhere is to get all of the things you need from one place and negotiate on the prices.

Always take your time, never rush or you will end up taking the first offer you get and end up regretting it and spending more money than you need to.

Gone are the times now where in the shops you just pay the price that is on the shelf and that's the end of it. With the ongoing treacherous economic climate that Great Britain still lie in, sales are constant and offers are always rife. So never take the first price that comes along. There is always the prospect of taking some free warranty or guarantee cover for items, if you cannot get something off the price of the actual goods.

# 22. CLAIM ALL ELIGIBLE EXPENSES

There are several ways in which an individual can claim for certain expenses and allowances that they may be entitled to. So you must always try to make yourself aware of what you can and cannot claim for.

One of the most common ways of claiming is the work uniform tax rebate. Although like most of the loopholes and rebates that are available to most of us, many people are not aware of them.

The work uniform tax rebate is available to all employees that are required to wear a uniform to work, and in order to complete their work. The idea of the rebate is to provide help with peoples extra laundry expenses due to the added amount of clothing that need to be washed and maintained.

Many people have been able to claim upwards of £300 back on their laundry expenses, as you are able to claim against your previous six years of employment. This is subject to you being able to provide details of those occupations; such as job title, works address, why you are not able to wear the uniform outside of work, if your employer makes any contributions towards the cleaning and maintenance of the uniform and the dates of employment in each eligible role for the tax in the previous six years.

For full details on how to claim, these are all available from HMRC.

## 23. PETS

Now this is also a bit of a strict one, but if you are going to be serious about saving money and be disciplined with most areas, then it should be pretty easy to abide by this money saving rule too.

Owning any kind of pet will cost you a lot of money, especially the standard domesticated animals such as cats and dogs, and then even the smaller critters like hamsters, gerbils, rabbits and rats.

Animals are a big commitment at the best of times, as well as also being a large financial commitment. Cats and dogs generally need to be insured, as the cost of broken limbs and illnesses are usually quite crippling.

So if you already have pets, make sure you get some pet insurance that covers for all possibly hugely expensive injuries. Using the same principle of saving as with other insurances, make sure that you do your research and compare all of the prices that you get, and then negotiate further on the best policy price that you get. Once you've nailed down the best quote, pay for the policy all up front and then its dealt with and at the back of your mind, knowing you have some protection incase the worst happens.

For the rest of you that don't already have any pets, or are thinking about getting one – don't! Seriously think about the commitment first that you are making and the financial implications that are involved, especially if you are looking to save money towards a house etc.

## 24. INVEST YOUR MONEY IN ISA'S AND PREMIUM BONDS.

This is when what you do with your money starts to get serious. It is extremely important to invest your money wisely in the modern day so that you can maximise what you have, and so that you are not penalised later on in life by the tax system.

So this is why it is important to steer clear from Stakeholder Pension Schemes, avoid Employee Pensions at work and keep hold of your money in the present, so you know exactly where your money is, and where it is going to end up in the future.

It is a fact that you are taxed on your income, and it is also fact that you are taxed on the eventual pension income, which is the same money that you were taxed on originally. So why be taxed twice on the same money, when you can have 100% control of it in the present and manipulate where it goes and when.

If you are wanting to invest a large sum of money, notably in excess of £30,000, it would be advisable to deposit it by way of purchasing Premium Bonds which are a tax free haven for your money, and can be claimed for no fee at any time, with the bonus of the chance of winning cash prizes each month.

It is a very easy process to manage, anyone can buy them and there are no restrictions whatsoever apart from the £30,000 per person limit. Although you will be able to get around this if you are investing as a married couple for instance, as you will obviously be able to invest double, £30,000 in each name.

As well as being very easy to invest, Premium Bonds are just as easy to withdraw the money. You just need to fill out a redemption form and state exactly how much you would like to withdraw from your Premium Bonds account and the HMRC will send you a cheque for the amount.

Another important savings and deposit scheme to enter into, along with your standard current accounts, is to have an instant access cash ISA account open for tax purposes in order to save vast amounts of money. A standard ISA has an annual deposit limit of £5,400 with the additional benefit of interest.

Cash ISA's are an excellent way of being able to save large sums of money tax free within your personal annual allowance. There are various types of ISA's available on the financial market from the banks and building societies which will offer various rates of interest for your investments.

Cash ISA's are fast becoming a trusted and reliable source of savings, as well as now being used more and more often as a repayment vehicle for endowment mortgages.

The main benefit of the ISA's being that you can withdraw the money from the account whenever you need to, bearing in mind that you cannot add more than the annual allowance into the account to top it up after.

The ISA's are now proving to be the successor to the original endowment policies for endowment mortgages which were widely misrepresented and sold to consumers back in the 1990's.

## 25. PAY IN FULL & UP FRONT FOR ALL INSURANCE POLICIES.

With car tax and car insurance premiums always on the rise, as well as life insurance policies and buildings and breakdown cover, it is always wise to get the money together first and pay it all off in one go.

This way you get an automatic lump sum discount for paying it all off at the start of the policy, as well as knowing how much money you can budget for other costs to come.

Understandably this is a much more difficult method for people to be able to raise the money required up front, but this is where people need to budget and put money aside so they can afford to do so.

One of the best ways to spread the cost as much as possible is to stagger your policies across the year if this is possible for you to do. One of the worst things can be large sums of money coming out of your bank account all in the same month, so its prudent to save yourself the headache of trying to source all of the money in one go, and to try and spread the cost over the course of a whole year.

## 26. DO NOT HAVE UNNECESSARY INSURANCE POLICIES.

Quite a common misconception within the consumer insurance industry is one that many more insurances are compulsory than actually necessary.

One of the most popular examples of this is the Contents Insurance for your home. This is something which is especially important to remember if you are on a tight budget and need to maintain control of all of your regular out-goings each month. Whereas your Buildings Insurance for your home is compulsory and required by law, the Contents Insurance is not.

Although it may be considered a risk every time you refrain from taking out an insurance policy, you have to weigh up the pros and cons and judge each one based on its merits. So with regards to Contents Insurance, it is an idea to look at it a different way. If you are willing to accept a possible loss in the event of your home being burgled for the sake of paying out a large insurance policy that may or may not cover it, save yourself the money and cross that bridge when you come to it.

It can sound like a maverick attitude towards insurance, but with so many insurance companies wriggling out of paying towards losses due to theft and damage, most of them are not worth taking out in the first place. So you may as well keep the money and save it for other purposes, or for a possible rainy day for when you might actually need it. This way, you can try and keep back as much capital as possible.

Many other insurances which we all know that are not compulsory but are still taken out include mobile phone insurance. Mobile phone insurance is one of the worst value for money policies that are offered to us as consumers. These insurance companies will try in any way as much as they can to get out of paying to cover the cost of phone repair or maintenance.

One of the most common problems occurred is the screen breakage cover. The vast majority of new smartphones which operate on a touch screen facility are condemned as useless and cannot be used properly if their screen cracks in a crucial place, or if they are just dropped and do not work at all.

So the best way to cover the cost for this kind of repair is just to swallow it and pay for the repairs as and when they are required by going to your local phone repair shops, and do not take out any policies to cover them at all, as you will just be wasting your money completely.

It's always important to remember, try to retain as much money as possible. Have as less direct debits and insurances set up as possible.

Don't be ripped off by the big boys!

## 27. CHARITY SHOPS – DON'T BE SCARED

Charity shops, despite being a mainstay on our high streets, always seem to be one of the things that remain stigmatised and do not get as much attention as they should.

But due to growing economic strain and pressures on the average family, more and more people are finding charity shops to be a safe financial haven.

By using any left-over money that you may have from your personal monthly allowance, why not take a trip into your local charity shop and see what you discover?

Many everyday items can be found from them, such as clothes, furniture, toys, DVDs, CDs and ornaments.

There is a common misconception that the charity shops tend to only sell used, dirty and unwanted goods. This couldn't be further from the truth, you will be amazed by the kinds of things that people throw away and waste. The vast majority of clothes being almost brand new.

So it seems that this is an opportunity to save money that many of us are missing out on because charity shops are always pre-judged unfairly and don't seem to get the visitors that they should.

## 28. DON'T GO ABROAD, STAY IN BRITAIN FOR HOLIDAYS.

While the costs for overseas breaks are still high and the exchange rate is so poor, take advantage of last minute British breaks and explore the British Isles. There are several ways that you can save yourself plenty of money, but still feel as though you have been away on holiday and more importantly had a break from it all.

One of the options available to consider if you are looking for a cheap holiday is to check the annual offers in the red top newspapers, as they have the token collections facility. Normally this will instruct you to collect up to

10 tokens and for the price in the region of £40, send them off with your top five choices of destinations provided in the newspaper and wait for the paperwork to be sent through.

The accommodation for these cheap holidays provided via the newspapers are usually in Caravans and Lodges located in Holiday parks which can be found all over the UK, and are even offered in France, Spain and Italy. So for the region of £40 plus any taxes and expenses, this is really an option really worth considering.

The other alternative to ensure that you have a budget holiday is purely for breaks in the UK. Quite often you will find that budget hotels such as Travelodge will offer extremely cheap rooms, sometimes from even £9 per night, ranging up to £29 per night. So for a cheap city break anywhere in the UK, if you just budget accordingly and add the cost of fuel and food, you will have yourself a 2 or 3 night stay in a British City for less than £60.

www.ingramcontent.com/pod-product-compliance
Lightning Source LLC
Chambersburg PA
CBHW050522210326
41520CB00012B/2402